EFFECTIVE NEGOTIATION AND CONFLICT RESOLUTION
Strategies to Become an Adaptive Negotiator

Entrepreneurial Briefing Series
Vol. 1 – Briefing No. 102

Author: Mosi Dorbayani

Library & Archive Canada, ISBN: 978-1-7770720-0-1

Orenda Publications, Canada

First Edition: 2005, IFSI Ltd. IFSI Publications - Hungary, European Union. Revised, 2019, 2025.

Cover Image by: Victoria Borodinova

This book is dedicated to you.

Contents:

Introduction   1

Effective Negotiation:

Part 1: Negotiation is a process, not an outcome.   3

Part 2: An Adaptive Negotiator secures commitments.   10

Part 3: Behind barriers lie choices.   16

Part 4: Persuasion is the key to our success in life.   22

Part 5: It never pays off to be too confident.   33

Part 6: Do not walk without leaving a door open.   44

Part 7: Our culture shapes the way we see the world.   49

Conflict Resolution:

The principle of relationship.   56

Introduction to conflict resolution.   57

Conflict resolution strategies.   58

About Author   62

References   66

Introduction:

Negotiation strategies for conflict resolution from the realm of business, trades, and political economy can help parties mend their partnership, avoid the expense of a lawsuit, and even create value.

Just look at the recent global issues:

China and Global Economy: China's growing presence and importance in the global economy, and current trade war with the United States, is raising public and entities' concerns.

Using Trade to Address Climate Change: The World Trade Organization – The WTO, and the United Nations Framework Convention on climate change seem to be at conflict. The WTO governs trade, but not climate change regulations. Certain new trade restrictions are coming into conflict with measures enacted to address climate change. While such measures should benefit the environment, they should not put trades at risk. (wto.org)

Risks and Rights: Our increasingly digitized societies are facing privacy risks. The online privacy is a growing concern for the majority of global users around the world.

Global Refugee Crisis: The World Refugee Council - WRC, tries to encourage cooperation, enforce political accountability, raise funds and develop technologies to tackle the current global refugee crisis. But there are still plenty of factors, which are slowing down the efforts. (worldrefugeecouncil.org)

Renegotiation of NAFTA: The United States-Mexico-Canada Agreement - USMCA, is intended to replace the North American Free Trade Agreement – NAFTA, to create a modernized free-trade system between the three parties that addresses recent and emerging critical issues, such as the harmonization of regulatory systems, e-commerce and the protection of Intellectual Property - IP. But how USMCA can protect the IP rights, traditionally passed down knowledge and cultural expressions, while developing a knowledge-based economy?

The examples above, are among many conflicts that can affect all of us if they are not properly addressed and negotiated. And of course, negotiation is one of the fastest and cheapest alternatives to dispute resolution – not only in the context of international business or trades, but also for resolving interpersonal / political disputes. Therefore, understanding the significance of negotiation and its applications is essential for learners and practitioners alike.

In today's disruptive, highly interactive, multicultural world, negotiation – the ability to communicate with and influence others – has become more important and even more complex than ever.

Whether you negotiate across continents or conference tables, this briefing aims to expand your leadership competencies, and to furnish you with insights to become an adaptive negotiator, who can function in any given situation.

PART 1

"Negotiation is a process,
not an outcome."

*E*ffective negotiators are highly adaptable. They do not stick to static and strategies all the time. Skillful negotiators are highly vigilant throughout the whole process of negotiation – from beginning to the end and are constantly absorbing information on their counterparts. Absorbing information such as:

- Habits.
- Speaking patterns.
- Presentation patterns.
- Personal style.

Skilled negotiators monitor themselves as well and make certain that they avoid reactions to choices that their counterpart presents.

But what are the choices? Well, a negotiator may choose whether to take an *Integrative* or *Distributive* approach to negotiation – or *somewhere in between the two.*

- **Integrative Negotiator:** Is the one who focuses on the other side's needs and interests.

- **Distributive Negotiator:** Is the one who has no regards for the needs or interests of the other side.

If you look at this in terms of a continuum (see Figure 1), at one end is purely Distributive negotiation in which the negotiators at the end of the spectrum are addicted to winning. They even may lose their original goal and aims of others in return of being able to say, "I WON".

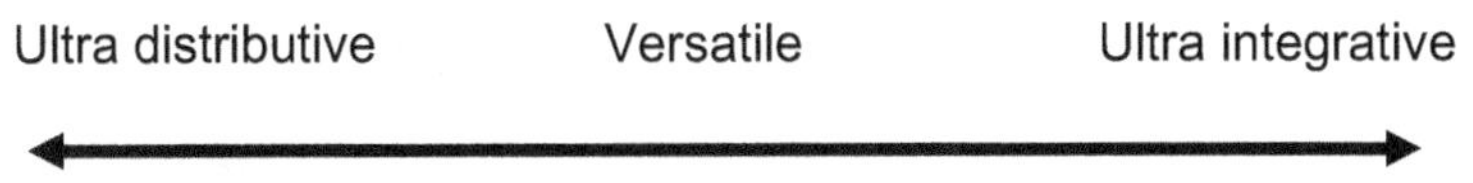

Ultra distributive   Versatile   Ultra integrative

Figure 1. A continuum of Competition & Cooperation.

I remember once a businessman who had just returned from a negotiation in Russia, proudly shared me that he had not let them "get the best" of him. He described how he had stood his ground, pushed his goals, and refused to back down. I asked if he had been successful. He replied, *"I did not get what I wanted, and they did not get what they wanted – but now they understand that I am not going to back down, that I intent to win. That is important, so in that respect, I won."*

That businessman was never invited back to Russia as for his habitual focus on winning and disregarding the process of give and take, which is requisite to "WIN". At the other end of the continuum is purely integrative negotiation in which the negotiators at the end of the spectrum are almost exclusively on the needs and interests of the other side. Ensuring that the other side leaves with a sense of having won is imperative to these negotiators and are willing to sacrifice a good deal to achieve it.

Although the more productive side of the continuum is usually the Integrative one, it is possible for negotiators to go far and give up too much to feel that both sides have attained something.

In one of my seminars, an officer complained of his supervisor, "He is a very nice fellow, but that is the problem. He wants to make everyone happy and satisfied, so we actually get nowhere."

Somewhere near the middle of continuum, moving as needed toward the Integrative or Distributive end – but never too far in either end are adaptable negotiators. They are so flexible that at their best, they are so well prepared in their goals prioritization that they know how much to give, how much to retain, and how much to do either – or both.

Adaptive negotiators are not committed to either 'win-win" or "win-lose". They know while the 'win-win' is typically preferable, understanding how to engage the 'win-lose' is what enables them to obtain their goals.

Adaptive negotiators do not memorize strategies, they rather practice *Versatility*.

They try to be more versatile than their less competent counterparts.

Total surprise is a rare experience for adaptive negotiators. Even when it does happen, they are prepared due to the fact that they trained themselves to adapt, to step back if necessary, to reassess negotiation conditions before making the next move.

Achieving 'versatility' needs a crystal-clear awareness of the basics and fundamental elements, which could be obstacles to successful negotiation.

Awareness of:

- Dangerous Assumptions;
- Usage of Questions;
- Measurement of Environment.

Let us now briefly look at each in turn.

Dangerous Assumptions: Try not to assume too much about the other side. Too much of assumptions can potentially get the negotiator far from the realities and facts of the situation. Do not assume very much that you know a person. If we understand ourselves as constantly evolving beings, then we must both recognize the need to continually get to know each other and continually appreciate the changes that have transpired.

Skillful negotiators do not impose commonality or specialty assumptions on others, they study them and try their bests to make sense of who they are, how they think, and what they need. Adaptive negotiators make a balance between observation and action, which is needed at the time of negotiation. Those negotiators who even put more emphasis on observation side, gain the advantage even in crisis.

Usage of Questions: Type of questions in negotiation is critical. Adaptive negotiators typically enter negotiations with prepared questions. Questions asked at the beginning of the negotiation must result in general information about:

- What the other person thinks will achieve;
- What expectations s/he has on each side's goals;
- Attitudes on key and fundamental issues;

- Interest in development or maintenance of relationship;
- Her/his own goals.

Open – ended questions such as 'How do you feel about X/Y?' Or 'What are you hoping to achieve today?' need to be asked in the early stages.

As negotiation progresses and proceeds, conditional questions become more applicable. These involve probing questions for specific information about proposals. Questions such as 'What would happen if we were...?' Or 'If we go ahead as you suggest, what will that mean for...?'.

Conditional questions do not pin down either side. They focus on hypothetical conditions. 'If we make a three-year contract, what would be the advantages or disadvantages for you?' This question does not specify that a three-year contract is the choice; it rather explores what the effects of such agreement might be. "What if?" questions are effective for not facing a direct disagreement, where "NO" might damage a relationship.

Questions are also tools of influencing the other side to participate more in the discussion. Skillful negotiators strive to do less than a majority of the talking and allowing the other side to make most of your side's points by asking questions that lead to the desired end. 'Have you considered approaching this form on point X/Y?' Or 'If you were us, would you take this approach?' Questions as such are somewhat leading type.

Measurement of Environment: Negotiations do not happen in vacuum. They are influenced by internal and external factors such as: Time pressure, Number of participants, Proximity, Location, etc. In an environment where human beings interact nothing remains completely static. Skillful negotiators know that power is not a static issue and it can change favorably if the conditions are managed appropriately.

Here the point is that everything involving in negotiation is subject to change – subject to another interpretation besides the easy or obvious one. A skilled negotiator starts negotiation with this mind-set. Bear in mind that: *Negotiation is a process, not an outcome.*

PART 2

*"An Adaptive Negotiator
always clarifies and secures
commitments."*

*C*ommunication in Negotiation would be for sure easier and smoother if both sides clearly and frankly articulated their types of interaction. People do not all the time talk, they simply engage in one or several types of talk. Types such as: 'Greetings', 'Discussions', 'Debates', and 'Arguments', etc.

One can hear sentences such as: 'Let's have a few words on this', 'Now we are here', 'Can we discuss this?' Usually they do not mention the types or sorts of talk, but act and operate on a non-stated understanding by both sides. Defining types of talk such as: 'Let's have an objective discussion', 'Shall we debate this objectively?', 'Personal attack is not my intention at all' are not articulated often.

Adaptive Negotiators look for assessing and controlling the sort of interaction that emerges during the negotiation so that make the process of interaction more fruitful.

Negotiation simply is not a series of unstructured back and forth free comments.

A skillful negotiator learns that *'How' of talk* (The types of language we select) is guided by the *'What' of talk* (The definition and category we place on).

Adaptive Negotiators are not open books. They control their actions and interactions to affect the types of language selected by their counterparts.

11

Moves of interaction are important to attend. Some negotiators assert themselves constantly. They use mostly Up moves ↑ while others are prone to acquiesce and make Down moves ↓ during their interactions.

For example:

Joe: You are a bit harsh on this projected planning document, aren't you? ↑

Peter: Are we? We were only trying to make a point there. ↓

Joe: Well, you sure didn't that. ↑

Peter: Did Ms. Lame say anything to you about it? ↓

Joe: She didn't have to. You should have paid attention to her expression. ↑

If you know that someone is inclined to be assertive, it is possible to manage interactions with that person. Once you are able to find out such inclination in direction, you are in a better position to manage or direct the other negotiator.

What is more, it is important to know your own inclinations in interactions, so that you do not fall into the trap of assumptions and predictabilities.

$\mathcal{P}$lanning of negotiation is an important factor to a successful one. Elements such as: Time pressures and overconfidence usually discourage negotiators from planning. Of course, the intention to prepare a plan by itself is not sufficient. One should know *What* it takes to prepare, is vital.

Before starting the interaction of negotiation, an Adaptive Negotiator will find out:

- The other side's needs and interest;
- The resources that are available to the other side;
- The authority of the other party to make decisions and agreements;
- Tactics that the other side is probably going to use;
- The point at which the other side might stop negotiating.

Of course, while negotiations are different in terms of required amount of planning and preparation, the above points can furnish you with a general guideline. A skillful negotiator who follows that guideline, can easier set the direction of the negotiation.

An Adaptive Negotiator bears in mind that negotiation is neither completely *'Competitive'* nor completely *'Cooperative'*. It is actually a *Combination*.

Competitive negotiators can potentially fail by being deeply involved in their positions and thinking to win while thinking little about the other side's needs. However, Cooperative negotiators who are popular too can have their own shortcomings as well.

Therefore, you need some steps for preparation:

1. Categorize your thoughts into three major issues of Primary, Secondary, and Tertiary.

2. Categorize the ideal outcomes in your Primary issue.

3. For each ideal outcome, develop contingency plan.

4. Have best alternative(s) to negotiated agreement.

Primary issue: ---------------------------

Ideal outcome is: ---------------------------

Contingency plan **A**: ---------------------------

Contingency plan **B**: ---------------------------

Contingency plan **C**: ---------------------------

Best Alternative: ---------------------------

5. Decide the importance of your outcome and determine how much emphasis you want to put on issues.

6. Decide about your opening tone (Concerned, Determine, Apologetic, etc.).

7. Develop Definitions, Metaphors, and Analogies to describe your position on each issue.

8. Determine what you will do in terms of non-verbal communication (body language) to enhance your emphasize of position, credibility, persuasion, maintenance of relationship, etc.

9. Determine how you will test your assumptions on the other side's interests.

10. Decide the way that you will link your interests with those of the other side.

11. Know your strongest point on each claim for each of your ideal outcomes.

12. Note what weaknesses your counterpart might point out about you and in that case how you will define your position.

13. Determine in each ideal outcome, what you are willing to concede that the other side may want and what you are unwilling to concede.

14. Determine what you will acquire if you are going to make concession.

15. Determine what kind of questions you will ask if the other side start focusing on your Tertiary issue.

16. Consider how you will make the other side involved in development of the solution.

An Adaptive Negotiator always clarifies and secures commitments.

PART 3

"Behind barriers lie choices"

A short negotiation about negotiation should take place to avoid diversions. Neglecting this step can waste the time and effort that would otherwise advice the negotiation.

Primarily you need to recognize: *Interests*, *Concerns*, and *Emotions* of your counterpart as they are detrimental factors of the desired outcome. That is why you need to establish a process guideline for the negotiation.

- Who starts first;
- Order of topics to be addressed;
- Time for each topic;
- Issues that should not be discussed during the negotiation.

I usually get this question that: *"What if the primary claim/issue of our counterpart is different from us? How to bring their interest to meet ours?"*

Well, the answer is that the process of selecting and supporting a Primary issue/claim is essential to a sound negotiation.

```
┌─────────────────────────┐   Therefore          ┌─────────────────────────┐
│ Data:----------------   │  ════════════▶       │ Claim/Issue:----        │
│        -------          │                       │        --------         │
└─────────────────────────┘   Since ▲            └─────────────────────────┘
                            ┌──────────────┐
                            │ Warrant:----- │
                            │    -------    │
                            └──────────────┘
                            Because ▲
                            ┌──────────────┐
                            │ Backing:------│
                            │    ------     │
                            └──────────────┘
```

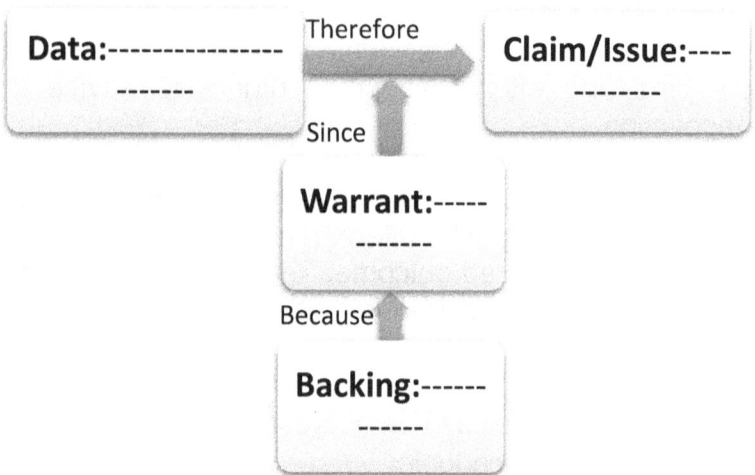

And it is important that Adaptive Negotiators devote as much as time as possible to get that right. Advocates in courtrooms, Debaters in universities, congresses, offices and backrooms prepare by learning their opponents' arguments and determining where their strengths and weaknesses are.

When selecting an issue/claim, you should ask:

- Why will my counterpart care about this issue?
- Is this issue about what they are likely to care most?
- Should I prove reasons why they should care before I introduce it?
- What are my backups claims if this one fails?

- What is the support for those?
- What is my order of priority for backup claims?
- Have I selected the strongest data, warrants, and backings for my Primary issue?
- Under what conditions will I drop a claim and move to another?
- Under what condition will I persist a claim and in what manner?
- What counterclaim are they likely to present?
- How will I process in each case?

It is very important when developing claims and their supports, to remain versatile by considering the possible counterclaims that other side may introduce. This is mentioned because it is not simply enough to have strong claims, data, warrant, and backings. Like a salesman you should be prepare for rejection. Therefore, have other supports claims available, so that if one door is closed, you can enter the other one.

Let us imagine this as a house. Majority of people's approach to a house is at the front door. When they receive no answer, they may ring the bill or knock again or simply leave. In this manner plenty of negotiators give up easily. They are early leavers. (See Figure 2)

Figure 2.

But a good negotiator is not easily satisfied. They assume that perhaps someone is in the backyard or doing something that do not let them to hear the bill or knock at the door. So, they check out the assumption. (See Figure 3)

Figure 3.

Meanwhile an Adaptive Negotiator examines all the possibilities. (See Figure 4)

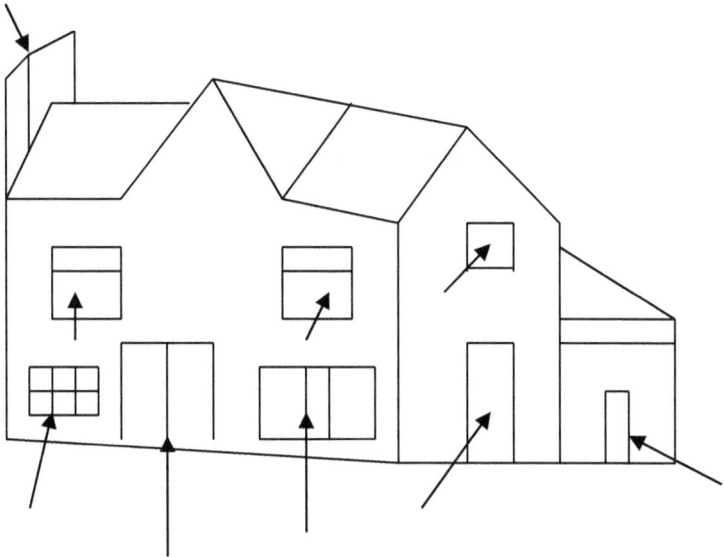

Figure 4.

Once you start to practice this form – you are not easily satisfied – you will make progress toward mastering negotiation skills.

Bear in mind that *behind barriers lie choices.*

PART 4

"The art of persuasion is the key to much of our success in life."

$\mathcal{S}$tyles of Negotiation are varied in general terms, but we can categories them into four: 'Analyzer', 'Motivator', 'Achiever,' and 'Mediator'. Let us now see the features of each:

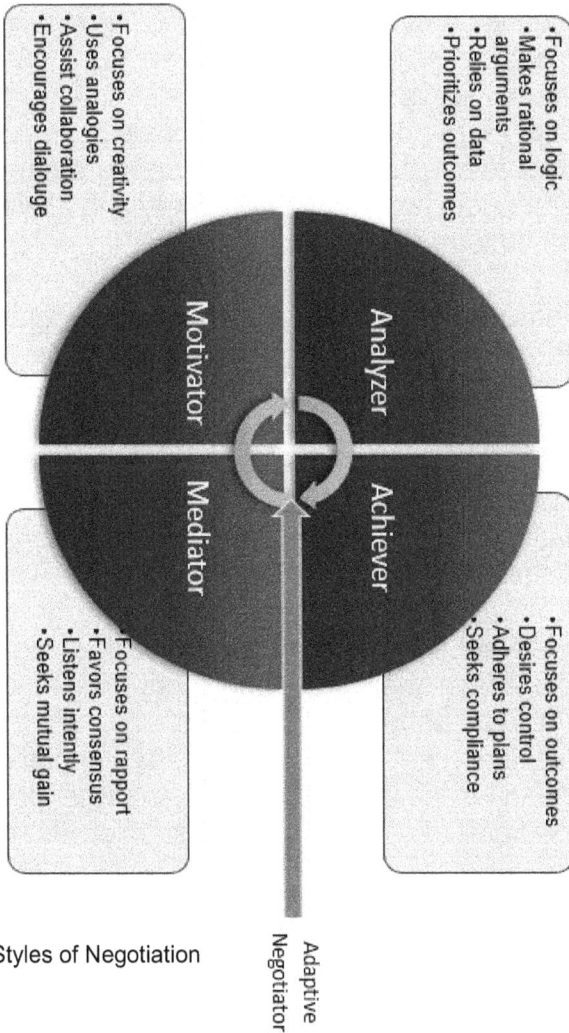

Figure 5. Styles of Negotiation

Achiever and Analyzer mostly employ hard tactics. Achiever mostly uses the hard tactic because they want to move things along, while Analyzer do so due to the fact the data appears to support their point of view.

Motivator and Mediator more likely use soft tactics. Soft tactics emphasize friendliness and create a sense of obligation and indirect approaches to 'persuasion'.

Style stretching is an important ability. It is important to know and learn how to communicate with an Achiever, if you are a Mediator: how to avoid boring them with your concerns about making people happy and how to phrase ideas so that they will listen.

If you are stuck in a Motivator style, your argument may be ignored when an Analyzer needs data, not dreams to get persuaded.

If you often face difficulties during the negotiation, you may want to consider that it may be due to your negotiation style – rather than issues related to the negotiation itself.

Adaptive Negotiators stretch their style and usually move about to adjust their style and strategies to effectively meet the style of their counterparts.
After setting up the structure of the negotiation and positioning issues in ways that assist further persuasion, now you need to consider the 'Persuasion Strategies'.

Persuasion strategies are also known as 'Compliance-gaining Strategies'. Researchers in this field, have made a list of persuasion strategies, which shows people selectively use them in variety of situations. Of course, people's abilities to learn and effectively use such strategies are widely vary; however, Adaptive Negotiators are aware of their options, and the application of such strategies.

For instance, engineers persuade other engineers by using different strategies then those they use with clients and blue workers. Teachers persuade students in ways different from those they use to persuade each other.

On persuasion, researchers Kathy Kellerman and Tim Cole (1994) compiled a long list of compliance-gaining strategy definitions, which here after I share some of them:

- **"Actor Takes Responsibility:** Try to get to comply by stating your willingness to help them or even work on the request yourself. *That is to gain their compliance by offering to do it yourself as a means of getting them to do what you want.*

- **Altercating** (Negative): Try to get others to comply by pointing out that only a person with negative qualities would not comply.

- **Altercating** (Positive): Try to get others to comply by pointing out that a good person with positive qualities would comply.

- **Altruism:** Ask them to *give you a hand* out of the goodness of their heart – just do it for you.

- **Assertion:** Forcefully state what you want. Demand (command) them to comply.

- **Audience Use:** Ask them in front of other people as a way to back up your request.

- **Authority Appeal:** Use or rely on a position of power.

- **Aversive Stimulation:** Do things they do not like until they agree to comply. Bother them until they do what you want.

- **Bargaining:** Negotiate a deal where you each do something for the other so that every party gets what it wants.

- **Benefit** (Other): Point out how it helps people other than themselves if they comply.

- **Benefit** (Self): Tell them you personally would benefit if they do what you want.

- **Challenge:** Challenging, provoking, stimulating, tempting, or galvanizing them to comply.

- **Compliment:** Praise them, their abilities, or their accomplishments to gain their compliance.

- **Compromise:** Make a concession to them so that they will make their concession to you and do what you want.

- **Cooperation:** Be cooperative and collaborate with them; try to gain their compliance by offering to discuss things and work them out together.

- **Criticize:** Attack them on a personal level to get them to do what you want.

- **Debasement:** Act pitiful and pleading. Debasing, demeaning, degrading, devaluing, humiliating, or lowering yourself so as to deprive yourself of esteem or self-worth to get them to do what you want.

- **Deceit:** Try to get others to comply by misleading, lying to, or deceiving them.

- **Direct Request:** Simply ask or state what you want without giving any reasons for them to comply.

- **Disclaimer** (Norm / Rules): Downplay or restrictions and constraints that might prevent them from doing what you want them to do. Point out that otherwise applicable procedures, rules, norms, or expectations should be broken in this instance.

- **Disclaimer** (Other): Downplay or disavow the ability of anyone else to comply with your request. Point out that other people cannot help you or do what is needed.

- **Disclaimer** (Self): Downplay or disavow your reason for asking. Indicate that:

  1. You do not want to make a bad impression or have bad intentions;

2. You do not really want to make the request and are doing so reluctantly;

3. You simply have no choice but to make the request.

- **Disclaimer** (Target): Recognize, acknowledge and sympathize with why they may not want to comply. Try to gain their compliance by indicating that:

    1. You understand and are aware of their reasons, feelings, and abilities;

    2. That you are sensitive to their needs and concerns even though you must ask them to do what you want.

- **Disclaimer** (Task): Downplay what you are asking them to do. What you want them to do is not what they think it is and should not pose a problem; it is not awful, difficult, or dumb.

- **Disclaimer** (Time): Downplay or disavow being busy as a reason to refuse your request. Point out that presently there is – or shortly will be – enough time for them to do what you want.

- **Duty:** They should fulfill their obligations, responsibilities, and commitments that they have.

- **Equity:** Being fair, just, and impartial means that they should do what you want.

- **Esteem** (Negative) by Others: If they do not comply, other people will think worse of them.

- **Esteem** (Positive) by Others: If they do what you want, other persons will think better of them.

- **Esteem** (Positive) by Actor: You will think better of them if they comply.

- **Expertise** (Positive): In the natural course of things, good outcomes will occur if they do what you want.

- **Hinting:** Indicate indirectly what you want, hoping they will figure it out and comply even though you never come out and really say it.

- **I Want:** Try to get others to comply for no reason other than you want them to.

- **Invoke Norm:** Indicate that they would be out of step if they fail to comply – prod them to conform to what others have, do, or desire.

- **It Is Up to You:** Tell them that the decision is theirs to make, and it is up to them.

- **Logical:** Make logical arguments, Use reasoning, evidence, facts, and data.

- **Moral Appeal:** Appeal to their moral or ethical standards. Let them know what is right and what is wrong.

- **My Concern for You:** Refer to your regard for, considerations of, interest in, and feeling for them.

- **Nature of Situation:** Be attentive to the situation or circumstances you find yourself in; then gain compliance by taking note of the appropriateness of your request in the situation.

- **Negative Affect:** Be really negative: Express negative emotions, act very unfriendly, or act displeased to get them to do what you want.

- **Not Seek Compliance:** Make no attempt to get others to do what you want.

- **Persistence:** Persevere (continue) in your attempts.

- **Personal Expertise:** Refer to your credibility. Try to gain their compliance based on your experience, know-how, trustworthiness, and judgment.

- **Positive Affect:** Be really positive: Express positive emotions, act very friendly, and create an appealing impression. Charm them into doing what you want.

- **Pre-giving:** Do positive and nice things for them in advance of asking them to do what you want. Give them things they would like and only afterward make your request.

- **Promise:** Offering to give them a reward or something they would like if they do what you want.

- **Promote Task:** Promote the value and worth of what you want them to do. Identify positive qualities of the thing: It is important, meaningful, rewarding, enjoyable, and so on.

- **Self-Feeling** (Negative): State that failure to comply will result in an automatic decrease in their self-worth. They will feel worse about themselves.

- **Self-Feeling** (Positive): State that they will feel better about themselves if they do what you want.

- **Suggest:** Other suggestions about what you want from them. Subtly propose an idea that indirectly points out and describes what you want them to do.

- **Surveillance:** Indicate your awareness and observation of what they do. Refer to your general vigilance, surveillance, scrutiny, or monitoring of their behavior.

- **Third Party:** Have someone else intervene and ask them for you.

- **This Is the Way Things Are:** Refer to rules, procedures, policies, or customs that require them to comply.

- **Thought Manipulation:** Convince them that the request you are making is really their own idea.

- **Threat:** Say you will punish them if they do not do what you want.

- **Value Appeal:** Point to central and joint beliefs that should guide what they do.

- **Warning:** Alert them to possible negative consequences of their behavior.

- **Welfare** (Others): Tel them how other people would be hurt if they do not do what you want. The welfare of others is at stake.

- **Why Not:** Make them justify why should not comply. Point out that there are no real grounds for not doing so.

- **Your Concern for Me:** Refer to their regard for, consideration of, interest in, and feelings for you as reasons to comply." (Kellermann and Cole, 1994)

With view to the above, *the art of persuasion is the key to much of our success in life.*

PART 5

" It never pays off to be too confident of one's power position in negotiation "

*A*nticipating *persuasion obstacles* is a very important factor to a successful negotiation. It is something that must be done continuously and only before or at the beginning of the negotiation. (Zohar,2015)

In general, we can name followings as the obstacles:

- **Possession Obstacle:** Showing that they don't have required resources.

- **Imposition Obstacle:** Showing that accepting the request would impose on prior plans.

- **Inappropriateness Obstacle:** Showing that the requirement or request violates rule.

- **Source Responsibility Obstacle:** Showing that it is the requester's responsibility to care of the problem.

Let us here examined some samples on the above:

Possession: "We can't pay that much"

Response: "What can you pay at this stage / time / point?

Imposition: "Our timetable is full, that is not going to work for us"

Response: "Is there any day that is might allow you to at least try doing…?

Inappropriateness: "That is out of the question/That is too much to ask"

Response: "What things might I do to make even in your estimation?"

Source: "This is actually not our problem"

Response: "Perhaps not quite obviously so. But how we handle it significantly affect you"

Recalcitrance: "The answer is no" / "No, that's final"

Response: "We'd likely to respond the same way if we were you. But do you think there is another time when some part of what we are asking might be feasible?"

Furthermore, 'Evidence and Credibility' are essential once having the potential obstacles identified. So, the next consideration for persuasion is whether the other side is going to believe you know what you're talking about. Therefore, it is better to enter a negotiation with objective criteria.

The standards for objective criteria are higher these days because so many credible Internet – based information such as government, corporate, and nonprofit sites as well as search engines are available.

Followings can be considered as the sources for evidence:

- Research support;
- Expert opinion;

- Expert affiliation and/or support;
- Experience;
- Comparison;
- Analogies;
- Examples.

Let us now take a look at the role of 'Power' in negotiation.

Power has relatively a number of static indicators. They are rank, gender, age, reputation, status, intelligence, reputation, appearance, and even physical size.

The more powerful a person perceives him/herself to be, the less likely he is to listen to and follow the recommendations of people with less power. Moreover, persons who perceive themselves at a power disadvantage in negotiation tend to monitor their actions more carefully.

It never pays off to be too confident of one's power position in negotiation. After all, power advantages, even status, can be diminished.

Respect is crucial to negotiation. If the other side regards you as a fair and worthy counterpart or opponent, the outcome of negotiation is likely to be positive for both parties. However, if they are not fair – minded, it may be necessary to win respect based on ability to gain advantage.

If someone possesses more power, you might argue, shouldn't that person win?

Why, with supposedly greater power, would a person choose not to win? The answer relates to the subtle but important distinction between views of power as _owned_ or power as _crafted_.

Here are a few important rules for the use of power during negotiation:

- Establish credibility.
- Do research.
- Do not have all the answers.
- Do not argue over the small stuff.
- Create dependence.
- Use the power of who you know.
- Do not appear overbearing.
- Use your time strategically.
- Choose the context carefully.
- Use threat only as the last resort.
- Do not play the same power hand twice.
- Remain flexible.
- Familiarize yourself with the political background.
- Do not go to negotiation alone (As much as possible).
- Do not let yourself become flustered.
- Find the soft spot.

Let us now briefly look at each rule.

Establish credibility:

This rule can be easily misunderstood with that of showing off yourself to the eyes of other part. When one tries to show off the other may feel the need to push him/her down. Where you need to be shown off it would be better to be done by others who say favorable input on you or allow a team member to introduce you. It is also practical the other side is provided with a biography of you that describes your accomplishments or those of the team members well in advance the of the negotiation session.

Do research:

Have support for ideas. Make them compliment you that "He/She knows his/her stuff". The more well-read you are, the more prepared you will be to introduce negotiation information with which the other side may not be as familiar. Present your information in a constructive rather than disruptive manner and with an attitude of assistance rather than arrogance. Once the other side sees this it is more likely to be impressed. Negotiators who have done their homework bring a high degree of confidence to the table.

Do not have all the answers:

However it is important to do research and know the issues of negotiation entirely, it is not constructive to overly highlight your expertise. Many negotiators think they should:

A) Be right;

B) Be seen as right;

C) Make others feel that they must therefore be wrong.

In such case most people feel insecure and do not wish to be looked down on. An Adaptive Negotiators on the contrary tries to help other side remain confident that no matter what the issue of disagreement and no matter how heated the room may become, they respect the other party's accomplishments and position.

Do not argue over the small stuff:

Many negotiators have lost an entire deal by pushing hard on minor gains! Know what matters most to you, by studying and research.

Create dependence:

This is actually called Centrality Power. It comes from occupying central position in important networks. For example, when Senior Executives depend on central ones to gather information or make needed connections, the power of the central ones is enhanced. Here the following equation illustrate the relationship between the power and dependence:

Power A, B = Dependence B, A

The power of person A on person B is equal to the dependence of person B on A.

Based on this, a negotiator would do well to make sure that the other side depends on him or her for some valued resource. The resource may be information and or an idea on how make the other side look good to its superior at the end of the negotiation, or it might be simply respect.

The key to this is the constant question from yourself that: *'What do I have that the other side might want?'*

Use the power of who you know:

The one who has the marbles, connections, even charm and beauty can hold more power. Of course, one should know when to use connections, drop a name etc. If a person feels trapped or cornered will become defensive and that hardly bring a positive outcome.

Do not appear overbearing:

In negotiation, power does not accrue to the person who has the right answer or even the best one. People often respond better to those whom they believe to have some faults.

If you act like you have all the right answers, others will often do what they can to hinder you from achieving your goals. On the other hand, if you share credit, involve others so that they have a propriety interest in making solutions work, demonstrate competence, and allow others to take the lead now and then. In this case the chances for a successful negotiation will increase.

Use your time strategically:

Strategic use of time is crucial in negotiation. Especially in Western Societies in which people are convinced that time is money and should not be wasted. Indeed, time can mean money in negotiation but only when it is used wisely.

Many negotiators use to speedy negotiations. Getting the issue on the table and pressing for results. This conveys doubts that you might be under pressure or even that you are desperate.

Choose the context carefully:

The food, the room, the temperature, lighting, and seating are all critical to a positive outcome. When people really do not want to be there, you do not want to give them any additional reasons for not co-operating. The environment of negotiation is a powerful facilitator or inhibitor of negotiation's success.

Use threat only as the last resort:

Demands and threats often fail the negotiation to attain its optimal outcomes.

Threat is the act of a desperate negotiator, and desperation is an impression you should not want to give. When you resort to threat, you are no longer negotiator. In fact, you are engaging in coercion – a very different form of influence.

When reason does not work, where the people involved are clearly used to compelling others to do their biddings, veiled threat may become necessary. *A veiled threat is subtle and deniable.*

Do not play the same power hand twice:

If you use the same tactic more than once, be sure of what you are doing. An Adaptive Negotiator is the one who uses an extensive repertoire of strategies and tactics. You should not be predictable and easy to win over.

Remain flexible:

Rules determined our word choice, but rules are immutable laws. They are bendable rules and often learned differently by different people. We know that women speak differently than men and that various types of relationships call for different forms of interaction.

Organizational culture can influence the type of words used, styles of usage, length of conversations, accepted channels of interaction, and the norms for who can talk freely with whom. Once people move beyond their speech communities, they must learn to rethink what they sat, how they say it, and to whom.

Familiarize yourself with the political background:

When formulating a negotiation strategy, you should consider four types of political environments in which you or the other side may be operating.

- Minimally Politicized Arena.
- Moderately Politicized Arena.
- Highly Politicized Arena.
- Pathologically Politicized Arena.

In the next segment, we will briefly discuss the various political environments as mentioned above and continue viewing the rest of rules there.

PART 6

" Do not walk without leaving a door open."

$\mathscr{I}$n order to familiarize yourself with political background you need to study these:

- **Minimal Politicized Arena:** Is actually what you see is what you get. In this arena power possessed by those who are truthful and who demonstrate concern for not only their own outcomes but also those of other side. In this, one side's gain is hardly viewed as another's loss. Rules may be occasionally bent, and small favors given, but parties treat each other with regard.

- **Moderately Politicized Arena:** Is characterized by a greater acceptance of behind-the-scenes tactics. Most rules are formally sanctioned. People in this arena have organizational tolerance, rather than encouragement. In this, power is with those who are not flouting the rules but works largely within them. Those whose comments show a respect for rules, but actions and manners are getting things done.

- **Highly Politicized Arena:** Is the one in which conflict is frequent. Formally sanctioned rules are invoked when convenient, rather than being applied consistently. In this power goes to those whose tactics bring desired outcomes, even if formal rules must be broken and behind the scenes arrangements must be made.

- **Pathologically Politicized Arena:** Is characterized by frequent often long-lasting conflict. Most goals are achieved by going around the rules. Distrust is high and people spend a lot of time watching their backs. In this arena power goes to those who are manipulative and controlling.

Having the above overview on political background, let us continue with the rest of the rules:

Do not go to negotiation alone:

You may be the best negotiator, but that does not mean you must be out there with no background support. To advance an idea in negotiation, you need supporters who are either present at the table or whom you can mention. People are sometimes skeptical of the ideas of one person but more comfortable with those that have backers, especially when the backers are regarded powerful people.

Do not let yourself become flustered:

Start negotiation with determination to do so. The best negotiators are cool under fire. The more prepared you are, the more successful you'll be as a negotiator. Life is full of twist and turns, unexpected bends in the road. Negotiation is no different. If you cannot handle them, then you do not belong on the road.

Find the soft spot:

Adaptive Negotiators may disclose something about themselves that seems private or personal. This expression of trust often elicits a reciprocal of information from the other side. For example, mentioning that you have children when you know they do. Be patient and probing and you may discover that you are in a position of great power simply because you can fulfill an unspoken personal need that the other side desperately harbors.

Here I take the opportunity to emphasis that there are times when you need to be responsive to potential or real conflict. Here are some tips on how to respond:

- Maintain an event strain.
- Ask clarification questions.
- Reposition or frame the problem in positive or mutual gain manner.
- Link something, they believe or value to what you also believe or value.
- Emphasize what has been accomplished over what has not.
- Avoid pushing on small issues or those that will resolve themselves over time and later on.
- If style is involved, meet them halfway.

When an impasse is reached, perhaps you need to handle it by:

- Take a break to strategize.

- Reconsider the amount that might be accomplished at this meeting.

- Visibly lower your dependence on them or raise their dependence on you.

- Break the problem into parts.

- If the impasse is on substance, focus on process – how to proceed from here.

- If the impasse is on process as well, try the shared text approach.

- Keep power in your pocket. Be a lawyer behind the scenes, advising; negotiating; consequences that may obtain on other issues if agreement on this one is not made.

- *Do not walk without leaving a door open.*

PART 7

" Our culture shapes the way we see the world, what we think, and what we say."

Adjusting is an important factor for an Adaptive Negotiator. It is usually a question that: "Why am I supposed to be the one doing the adjusting? Or, why don't they adjust to my culture?

My answer begins with a question: "Do you want this negotiation to go well and to be successful?" The answer is always yes. Some add that yes, but the other part should want to go well too; therefore, the other side should do half the work in terms of cultural sensitivity. Each side should do half the work.

But here my view is: *You have to know enough about them to know what that half should look like*, and if they will not or cannot meet you halfway but rely on stereotypes, you will need to decide whether the negotiation is important enough for you to do the lion's share of adjusting or not.

An Adaptive Negotiator has a "Global Mind – Set". Cross-cultural agreement usually takes longer than those within a single culture. McDonald's negotiated for almost ten years to open its first restaurant in Moscow. (NYTimes, 1988)

Negotiating a joint venture in China takes an average of two years. In Latin America, delay of thirty minutes or more are to be expected before a negotiation gets started. In Middle East, there will be some time for tea before entering into negotiation.

In Spain business can be over dinner, which may begin at 10 P.M., and in Japan, a good deal of circling back to review an already discussed subject is likely to occur on a number of times. Time is not linear in these cultures. It is polychromic with no beginning or end. (Gwiazda, 2016)

Impressive data are less likely to elicit trust from a Japanese counterpart than attention to feelings and personal considerations. This does not mean that they do not want data but rather that in the absence of a positive relationship; the data may fall on deaf ears.

In Middle East, using an intermediary trusted by both sides accompanied by demonstrations of respect and generosity is often a promising avenue.

Attending to control concerns of Russian counterparts and endeavoring to assure them of respect is critical to trust. Do not expect friendship to be easily given.

A warm smile and a handshake aren't sufficient in most regions of the world. Trust, in North American style, is a function of staying on track, and not behaving in ways inconsistent with prior agreements finds meaning.

In cross-cultural negations, there are certain general rules, which you may need to follow.

Ten general principles for cross-cultural negotiation:

1. Before arriving for talks, learn as much as possible about each member of the other side's team. Know their interests and status concerns.

2. Be prepared for differences in concerns about time, punctuation, attitude, and logic process. In some cultures, agendas should be used as informal guidelines.

3. Remember that relationships are critical to success in most regions of the world. Treating contract as binding legal instruments can be insulting and detrimental to relationships (Particularly in China, Japan and Korea)

4. Do not automatically treat compromise as the answer to impasse, Esteem for this solution varies widely.

5. If you do not speak your counterpart's language, find a good interpreter and _practice with the interpreter_. When you meet with your negotiation counterpart, speak to the counterpart, not to the interpreter (Yours or theirs)

6. Be sure the others know your accomplishments and experience, but do not boast. You could send a biographical sketch in advance, along with some information about your company and some key points of the topics.

7. Be patient. If questions are repeated or topics reemerge, it may be a test of your knowledge, sincerity, or commitment to the work and the relationship.

8. Prepare and prepare. Think in terms of four stages of intercultural negotiations:

A) Relationship building;

B) Task-related exchanges of information;

C) Persuasion; and

D) Concessions & agreement.

9. If misunderstandings occur, slow thing down. Do not demand that the discussion return to a prior tone.

10. Use the strategies you have learnt here but be sure to balance attention to your goals with attention to your level of adaptation.

The final remarks on this segment:

Here I end this briefing with the following notes for you to remember:

- **Versatility:** Enter negotiation completely ready for surprises. Using assumptions but treating them a tentative. No matter how well you know the other side or person, the key is to gather intelligence in the service of developing and maintaining a versatile frame of mind.

- **Defining Goals:** Once you have identified interests, relevant issues, and their priorities, articulate for each of the high-priority issue one more ideal out-comes, contingency goals. Check the strength of the data, warrant, and backing that you have for each claim.

- **Setting the Agenda:** Develop and propose the order in which issues will be addressed and claims advanced. A good agenda avoids extensive discussions of clutter issues.

- **Framing:** Word your positions on key issues in ways that are memorable and persuasive. Use analogies, images, and stories.

- **Persuasive Opening:** First impression is crucial. Carefully consider how you will introduce issues.

- **Handling Conflict:** Conflict is natural in Negotiation. Resources are usually scarce, and often one or both parties believe that any gain for one is a loss for the other. It is important to treat conflict as a cue for change rather than as a threat.

- **Cross Cultural Divides:** When negotiators leave the relative comfort of their surroundings for other countries, they must pay greater attention to differences. *Our culture shapes the way we see the world, what we think, and what we say.*

Conflict Resolution

The Principle of Relationship

Undoubtably, 'mutual respect' is the key to any successful relationship. Having mutual respect is particularly important during negotiation, where cultural and linguistic differences may occasionally result in misunderstandings between the parties. Often such differences influence the perceptions and assumptions of individuals and how they bargain. (William & Berman (1982)

As mentioned in the previous segment, differences in gender may also play a role in the negotiating process, whether the parties are of the same or different cultural backgrounds.

Playing into stereotypes such as gender, cultural, physical or racial differences often reinforces misunderstanding between the parties. (Hill, 1990)

The ability to accept diversity demonstrates respect, and this in turn, will bring the required sensitivity in you during the negotiations – especially when addressing disputes.

By avoiding the stereotypes, you can enhance the relationship between the parties and reduce the chances of misinterpretation. (Thomas, 1993)

Usually in negotiations, both parties are aware of what their interests are, and they are willing to engage in a give-and-take process with the other party to come to an agreement. However, if their values are in conflict, the negotiation dynamics can change and become more complex and difficult to handle.

Introduction to Conflict Resolution

Conflict resolution is relatively a new study, emerging after World War II. Social scientists and political scholars on negotiation were leaders in establishing this field of study.

It generally refers to one of several different processes used to resolve disputes between parties, including: Negotiation (as discussed in the previous section), Mediation, Arbitration, and Litigation.

When there is a conflict, 'mediation' can play a crucial role. Mediation can allow parties to release their feelings and express their grievances. Mediators may work with parties together or separately to facilitate them reach to a sustainable resolution.

Sometimes in order to resolve a conflict, 'arbitration' is the best avenue. In arbitration, each party argues their case supported with evidence, then after careful and active listening, the arbitrator delivers a binding decision.

The other process to address a dispute or conflict is through 'litigation'. It typically involves a defendant facing off against a plaintiff before either a judge or a judge and jury. The judge or jury is mandated for weighing the evidence and making a ruling.

Conflict Resolution Strategies

As mentioned earlier, usually in negotiations both parties are aware of what their interests are, and they are willing to engage in a give-and-take process with the other party to come to a form of agreement. However, if their values are in conflict, the negotiation dynamics can change and become more complex and difficult to handle.

In conflicts related to values, beliefs, and identities, parties may not be willing to make any concession, which may help the other side, even if it would bring about a reciprocal concession that would be in their own interest.

Often 'cultural' or 'value-based' conflicts block continuation of negotiation; hence, conflict resolution tactics would be required to facilitated continuation of negotiation.

When facing 'cultural/value-based' conflict there are four practical steps that adaptive negotiators can take to adjust the situation, so that negotiation move forward in a constructive manner.

Conflict resolution is the process of resolving a conflict by meeting at least some of each party's needs and addressing their interests while demonstrating mutual respect.

Conflict resolution strategies often include:

- Establishing a rapport;
- Maintaining interests and values separately;
- Tapping into values; and
- Indirect confrontation.

Establishing a rapport: This is engaging in dialogue and building relationships through establishing rapport or common cause – hosting your counterpart to your side while trying your best to understand their interests and values during the negotiation.

Maintaining interests and values separately: Separate your counterparts from the issues and engage with them at the negotiation table. Determine what your counterparts hold as valuable in their positions at the table and negotiate accordingly without damaging their values.

Tapping into values: Often shared values and common interests can assist you to bridge the gap during the negotiation. This can bring you and your counterpart closer in terms of meeting your bargaining interests.

Indirect confrontation: Do not attack what your counterpart holds as their values. Your differences can be opportunities to create new values for both parties. Confront differences sensitively and always emphasis on mutual respect.

For any conflict resolution to be successful, first and for most we need to genuinely acknowledge that:

A. Sadly, we are all subject to our own perceptions of biased fairness, and;

B. We have tendency to think 'us versus them' during negotiations.

Therefore, we need to constantly keep our biased perceptions and hostile team affiliation checked at the door before sitting at the negotiation table.

Similarly, in managing conflict resolution, a mediator should act upon the followings without prejudice:

1. Conduct analysis of the parties and issues;

2. Bring the parties at the negotiation table to discuss their concerns;

3. Establish an agreement on what the problems are;

4. Help them to understand the costs of their former conduct; and

5. Facilitate them to see what the alternatives / possible options are.

Here I end this by emphasizing that, while conflict is often perceived as negative, uncomfortable and challenging, simply it doesn't have to be negative. Think about all the social and political changes, human rights, civil movements and prosperity that came about as the result of the conflict.

*"Coming together is a beginning,
staying together is progress,
and working together is success."*

Henry Ford

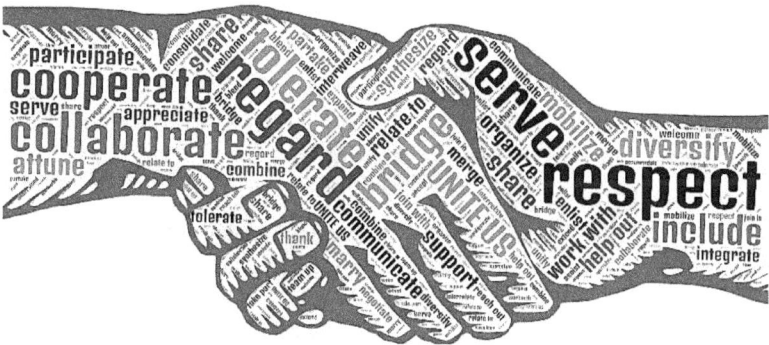

About Author:

Mosi Dorbayani, is a Canadian executive adviser, entrepreneur, educator, coach and consultant. He is author of 21 professional books and is a well-published international songwriter.

His executive experience, leading and collaborating with staff from 20 nationalities have equipped him with a global strategic understanding on the importance of cultural diversity and human capital. His passion for 'personnel / talent development' has enhanced many organizations, practitioners and trainees, and provided them with practical insights to face challenges of their constantly changing environment.

Educated at Harvard, Aston, Sunderland, Wolverhampton, and Salford Universities, Mosi is specialized in Business Economics, Management, International Law, Psychology, Cultural Diplomacy & Public Policy, and is a Chartered Professional in HR - CPHR, a Chartered Manager, - C.Mgr., a Chartered Psychologist - CPsychol (BPS), a member of Canadian Psychological Association, and International Bar Association (IBA - Law).

Follow Author:

LinkedIn: https://ca.linkedin.com/in/mosidorbayani

Instagram: https://www.instagram.com/MosiDorbayani

Full Profile: https://www.dorbayani.com/mosidorbayaniprofile

Also, from this author:

BUSINESS
SAMURAI
SKILLS AND STRATEGIES FOR
LEADERS &
ENTREPRENEURS

武

リーダーシップ

士

Available at
amazon

BARNES
&NOBLE

MOSI DORBAYANI

ENTREPRENEURIAL
BRIEFING
SERIES
Vol. 1, Briefing No. 101

Personnel / Talent
Development Strategies

Mosi Dorbayani, CPHR
Orenda Publications

TALENT-BASED ECONOMY

Talent Development & Leadership Succession Strategies:
A Sustainable Business Economics Act

MOSI DORBAYANI

References:

Gwiazda, B. (2016), P.30, 'Cross-cultural Communication', https://awl.edu.pl/images/en/Strategic_Partnership/Cross_Cultural_Commu nication_E-book.pdf, accessed 2016

Hill, E., P 337. 370, (1990), 'Alternative Dispute Resolution in a Feminist Voice', Ohio State Journal on Dispute Resolution.

Kellermann, K. and Cole, T. (1994), Classifying compliance gaining messages: Taxonomic disorder and strategic confusion. Communication Theory, 1, 3-60

New York Times, 1988, https://www.nytimes.com/1988/04/30/business/mcdonald-s-in-moscow-a-bolshoi-mak.html accessed 2005

Thomas, R. P 54, (1993), 'Colosi on Negotiation', Dubuque: Kendall/Hunt Publishing Co.

USMCA, https://ustr.gov/trade-agreements/free-trade-agreements/united-states-mexico-canada-agreement, accessed Nov. 2019

William, Z.; Berman, M. P 132. (1982), The Practical Negotiator - New Haven: Yale University

WTO,https://www.wto.org/english/tratop_e/envir_e/climate_challenge_e.ht m, and https://unfccc.int/resource/docs/convkp/conveng.pdf, accessed Nov. 2019

World Refugee Council, https://www.worldrefugeecouncil.org/sites/default/files/documents/WRC_C all_to_Action.pdf

Zohar. I. (2015), Procedia - Social and Behavioral Sciences 209, 540 – 548 Published by Elsevier Ltd. Creative Common.